Real Love *and* Good Sex

For Chronic Pain Patients and Their Partners

Written By Ken and Barby
Ken Ray Taylor and Barby Allyn Ingle-Taylor

Copyright © 2014 - BK Publishing

ISBN-10: 0615961010

ISBN-13: 978-0615961019

First Edition 2/14/2014

Real Love and Good Sex for Chronic Pain Patients and Their Partners

Real Love *and* Good Sex

For Chronic Pain Patients and Their Partners

Written By Ken and Barby
Ken Ray Taylor and Barby Allyn Ingle-Taylor

Real Love and Good Sex for Chronic Pain Patients and Their Partners

Contents

The advice and information contained in this book is for resource purposes only. This is not intended to replace or counter a healthcare provider's advice or judgment. Please consult your physician before taking any advice learned from this book, the internet, or found in any other educational medical material.

Real Love and Good Sex for Chronic Pain Patients and Their Partners

Foreword

For those who don't believe real love and sex can happen when you're ill, I know that it can.

Of the nearly 28 years together and 27 married, 12 of it was the result of the injury that caused me to develop reflex sympathetic dystrophy. In 2007, my husband had his first heart attack at age 38. At that time he had two stents placed in his heart and was diagnosed with diabetes.

In 2011, he had a second heart attack, surgery to correct a faulty stent and replace the other. In 2012 he had a quad bypass. During the years I've had several surgeries, over a dozen blocks and our family has had other health issues.

We both know not only our own disabilities but those of each other. Our love has held strong, we have endured much and still manage to say "I love you" several times a day. Intimacy doesn't always have to include sexual intercourse. Intimacy can include the sensual touch, loving caress, and the eye contact that makes your belly flutter. Falling into his embrace makes you feel warm and secure. I love the feel of his gaze luring you into his arms.

There are so many different ways to keep the spark alive when we are ill. When we experience intimacy endorphins are released into our body. This decreases pain perception and for those moments we are okay again. Some may not believe this, since it takes getting to that moment to understand.

It's okay to have sex and to even be happy in it. Many pain patients want to put the taboo on sex and believe it is wrong. I hear "OMG, I'm disabled I can't do it anymore" To that I say, NOT. Maybe we can't do all, but we can do some. I think that unless someone is an actual invalid it is possible. Even in that case it's still possible for the partner to give physical love. Ken and Barby share how to connect and reconnect in this book.

Chronic pain becomes a habitual affliction if you let it. This can be overcome with patience and practice. If you can suspend your disbelief long enough accept and envision that the real possibility of a loving, intimate and satisfying relationship is achievable with your partner, then you will be on your way to fulfilling each other's desires again.

Not every chronic pain patient is able to sleep with their partners in the same bed. My husband and I haven't for many years due to me having reflex sympathetic dystrophy and other health issues. This doesn't mean our love is any different than before. We make up for our physical limitations with creativity. For instance, I love to run my fingers through his hair because touch stimulates the senses for both of us.

When sexual intercourse isn't possible the precious act of intimacy still can be. Always keep the lines of communication open. Locking away your emotions, fears, needs and desires can lead to resentment and loneliness. Don't let the pain steal the relationship you long for with your partner. Work toward a solution that brings happiness to both of you. It is never too late to rebuild, rebound and rekindle the fire you each are longing.

Twinkle VanFleet

Preface

Yep, straight from the hip giving guidance to those who need it and new ideas to those that do not! This book came about because Barby and I were asked to do a small Valentine's Day segment on CBS for *The Doctors* TV show.

When we arrived at the studio the producer had us sit in front of a camera on a green screen set. We thought he was going to ask us questions that we would answer. However, what transpired was 18 minutes of us sharing our lives and talking about the importance of sex in a relationship.

The producer yelled action and asked us, "Why is sex so important in keeping your marriage strong". We introduced ourselves and began to answer the one question he had asked. We were prepared for this type of question to a certain extent. Two of the most asked questions we get from medical providers is do we maintain a sex life and what we would suggest for other patients in similar situations.

Both of us were thinking that there would be more questions and that the producer would cut us off at any moment. After talking for almost six minutes in technical terms we started running out of things to say. A normal person probably would have stopped at that point in the filming. Instead of stopping we continued on, knowing we were not supposed to stop until the producer told us to stop. We both ended up going into personal details about what we do to keep our bond emotionally and physically strong.

What came from this interview and talking to couples after it aired who are also going through similar situations was unexpected. We decided to put our learned wisdom on the subject into black and white print so we could help other couples who needed suggestions.

For the past year Barby and I have been writing this book together. Our relationship has grown even stronger through this process. Our hope is that you will find some useful information in this book that can be applied to your own relationship and that you create a real love that is lasting through the challenges of living with a chronic illness.

To help the reader of this book we alternated each chapter from our own perspective as a caregiver, patient, lovers, and best friends, except for the last chapter which we decided on together.

Enjoy!

Ken and Barby

Real Love and Good Sex for Chronic Pain Patients and Their Partners

Real Love

When we met Barby had just moved to Arizona and had already undergone surgery on her shoulder. She needed assistance and I offered to help my new neighbor. Little did either of us know that this was only the beginning of a chronic illness that neither of us had heard before that time. Later that same year Barby underwent a rib removal surgery after being diagnosed with thoracic outlet syndrome. She was not getting better. Her doctors thought that removing a rib would help the situation. With much surprise to us, they were wrong. It was another two years before she got the proper diagnosis of reflex sympathetic dystrophy. We had to figure out how to deal with these challenges on our own.

Barby, having a degree in social psychology, taught me about her studies of Bruce Tuckman. He created the stages of a relationship back in the 1960's and they still hold true today. These stages are tools that can be used to overcome life's challenges, tack health problems, and find solutions that work for both.

All relationships are based in these 5 stages. The five stages are forming, storming, norming, performing, and adjourning-transforming. Some stages such as storming, norming and performing may occur any number of times in a relationship before adjourning-transforming due to a severe health crisis, split of the relationship or death of a partner.

In the forming stage you are coming together for the first time. You begin the process of learning about each other as well as challenges, expectations, and how you are going to organize your relationship. It is an information gathering stage where you can explore and see if you would like the relationship to continue and on what level.

The hardest stage to get through and remain in the relationship is storming. We all come into a relationship with expectations and ideas of things we want to achieve. This is the time that the couple critiques, confronts and debates each other in an effort to decide on how they will partner moving forward. I am sure we have been through this stage a number of times and Barby can attest to that. This time in the relationship can be unpleasant if one or both partners don't approach it in a positive manner. Many relationships break up in this phase because they simply can't compromise on expectations.

For those couples who make it through the storming phase they really begin to function. Roles and responsibilities settle into place and you begin to work as a couple for a mutual relationship. This is known as the norming stage. You really get to know your partner in this stage. Most couples that make it to this stage stay in it for a while and revisit it several times throughout the relationship as it grows through the years.

I have always referred to longtime couples as an 'old married couple'. This is the performing stage of a relationship and obviously not all couples make it to this stage. This is what we strive to achieve. When you can finish each other sentences, are knowledgeable in deep aspects of your partners' beliefs and have accepted them. There are also those couples we strive to be like where they go through this stage multiple times in a relationship. For example, a couple has been together for 10 years. The husband becomes ill with cancer and a pivotal change occurs in the relationship. They go back to storming and norming stages. One of two things happen. Either they stay together and strong, or they split up. When they stay together it makes their performance stage that much better.

The final stage occurs either at the point of a break up or your relationship is transforming due to a new dynamic or challenge such as children and elderly parents coming into the relationship. Many times when you are breaking up or adjourning, you are filled with sad or negative emotions. It can be a difficult time and feel similar to mourning a loss of someone who has passed. Other times it means that your situation changed and you are going to cycle back through some of the other stages. Understanding this stage during a cycle helps you stay positive and strong making it easier to come through it together, just to do it all over again.

We flew past the forming and storming stage of our relationship very quickly. We were well into the norming stage when we had to stop and talk about the future and what expectations we had for each other as a romantic partner putting us back in the storming phase. Once we knew that Barby would be facing this health challenge for the rest of her life, I began to ask myself a series of questions. Could I be ready for this? Do I want to be ready for this? Does the benefits of our relationship outweigh the hardships we will face? I had to come to a realization on each of these issues before I could commit to her again with the new set of expectations.

I had to decide if I could manage spending my life with someone who may deteriorate physically to a point of total need. Would I be able to handle this situation when it comes down to it, and more important, did I want to? By this time, we were in love with each other and adding emotions to a complicated situation. Finally in May 2005, Barby was properly diagnosed with RSD. This was two years into our relationship which had grown from neighbors to friends to lovers.

This diagnosis was a test on relationship and a new starting point for us. It seemed as if things fell together once we had the diagnosis, yet the set expectations of the future became unknowns. We had to start over with our communication process to set appropriate expectations for what we both were willing to do. We also talked about how important it was to communicate with each other on how each of us is doing. We realized that both of us are going through the same hardships. We both experienced a loss of friends, family support, and finances.

Communication and setting realistic expectations upfront can help a couple cultivate a healthy loving relationship. Being able to effectively communicate helps you work out problems, keeping resentment manageable and keeping you strong as a couple when changes are needed. Simply put, pain changes relationships. If this is not addressed the bond breaks. The intimate bond doesn't have to end because of the pain. We both chose to fight for the best relationship that we could have by effectively communicating.

It is important to find enjoyment with your spouse. For instance, we would limit participating in social events because of unwanted stress and the increase in pain levels. We also kept in mind that different activities will interest me and not her. For instance, Barby is not that interested in the Ancient Aliens series and I don't love *Dancing with the Stars*. We choose to watch these and similar shows together as a way to bond and stay close. Barby also decided that she would participate in some activities I enjoyed even when it may cause an increase in pain. We just had to plan and prepare so that before and after the event she had time to rest and recuperate. Living with pain may mean you are choosing to participate in activities you would not normally do because you may experience a temporary increase in pain. That doesn't mean push yourself to the edge, rather find another way to accomplish the activity. If it is a birthday party, go for a short time so you can be there for the special event. You really have to look at hurt versus harm. Don't let the fear of pain interfere with important life events including sexual relations. Understanding the difference between hurt verses harm will broaden your activities and the scope of your relationship. Do nothing that will intentionally harm yourself as it will cause resentment towards your partner. Putting yourself in a harmful situation will cause you to withdraw from your partner emotionally and create trust issues. It is very important to not cause trust issues with your partner.

A goal to keep your communication strong will assist in keeping the love strong. Use technology to stay connected. Using email, text, social media, and calling each other provides an additional way to participate in the relationship. Don't be afraid of trying something new. Let the past be just that and learn from those mistakes. Focus on how you can stay connected with new goals. You do not have to isolate yourself just because you can't do all the things that you used to do. Remember, hurt verses harm. Work to create new roles and redefine your relationship to a point that is beneficial for you.

Barby and I decided to put it all out on the table; finances, chores, sex, extended family relations.

Everything was up for discussion and negotiation. A true connection is more than just your activities together in public. Connect in a strong and constructive manner on a personal level. This means getting through challenges in a positive, productive, and understanding process. If your partner is taking on new tasks because you are no longer able, there can still be a give and take. In our case I had to take over all the physical chores around the house. Barby took on the less physical activities and coordination of our daily activities. For example, paying bills, coordinating appointments, and online grocery shopping.

The key to real love is communicating. You will see this theme throughout the book. It may seem like a no-brainer but for your relationship to work you must communicate on the same level. Do so with respect and always keep in mind the love you share. Once you address the root cause of your pain, exploring possible treatments and seeing a pain specialist regularly will help with setting the proper expectations. Search out coping techniques that work for you and develop ways to get through the pain together as a united unit. When I come up with something that helps Barby it lets her know that I am thinking of her. For example, putting a stack of pillows at the end of the bed keeps the covers off of her feet. Nothing says 'I love you' like helping a person reduce their pain level. Be creative, there are many things you can do like this without spending a lot of money.

Barby's mentality is the more she can do herself, the better. And if there's something that she really can't or shouldn't do she asks for help. Barby has a positive approach to life and to facing this difficult challenge. Her positivity has made it possible for me to feel comfortable as her partner in life. I could not survive in a relationship that was constantly negative while facing a chronic disease with my partner. I let her know that she had to be assertive about her needs. She does this with a good balance so that she is not too demanding yet receives the assistance she needs. This positive approach to life is helpful in keeping our romance alive, even when she is having a very high pain day. This is an example of hurt verses harm. When the person is having a good day with their pain levels they may try to do too much. This causes harm because their body reacts negatively and they become physically unable to be intimate with you. When having a low level pain day set a goal to be intimate with your partner. Know your physical limitations so you do not cause harm to yourself and your relationship.

Rekindling Romance

Prior to my relationship with Ken I learned that you don't have a marriage without sex unless both partners honestly feel happy and satisfied in their relationship without sexual intimacy. Finding a partner to agree to a life with no sexual intimacy is rare. It is true that I don't feel sexy every minute of every day due to the pain. I learned there are ways to have a sexual relationship that is romantic even through the pain I live with on a daily basis. I realized having a sex life helps me with the pain levels.

If I was to lose my sexual connection with my husband I would work to regain it. I would start by talking with Ken. As any tough discussion I would start the communication process in the living room or in a neutral setting. I found we have the best conversations when 'I' is used to describe my feelings. Doing so helps keep stress, pressure and anxiety off him and vice versa. An example is, "I love when you hold me close; it makes me feel cared for". This is a positive way to state how you are feeling versus a comment like 'You must not love me because you never hold me close'.

Many times rekindling the romance is successful with proper communication. Maybe your partner is afraid of causing you pain. Keep in mind the things done out of kindness are a way of showing affection. These things can't be overlooked or taken for granted. Let them know you are still interested and willing to have intimacy. This can put your partner at ease. It is easy to jump to conclusions as to why your partner has stopped touching you. The reason is usually not that they lost interest in sex or in you. It is usually a lack of communication and can be fixed.

Ken and I had to have the conversation, what would make this more enjoyable for you? We had to experiment and try new things and get out of the 'norm' of traditional sex positions because it was too painful and not enjoyable for me. I believe that people with chronic pain, and those who love them, don't need to resign themselves to a lifetime of celibacy. The subject can be approached from several angles, but the main lesson from health professionals and strong couples is communication.

Communicate with your partner and your doctor or psychologist when needed. For us, our primary care doctor brings it up at every appointment. But if your doctor doesn't bring it up for you, don't be embarrassed to bring it up to them. They may have some great suggestions for you. They may be able to relate the lack of sexual desire to a complication of a medication you are taking. The provider can also validate that low libido is a common consequence of chronic pain.

Try keeping track in a pain diary so you can remember the details. Record at what point during intimacy pain occurred/increased or what the circumstances were surrounding an instance when your pain subsided. Understanding the underlying issues and complications can help you gain control of your intimacy.

There are techniques that a therapist can provide that will help a patient normalize their symptoms which can help boost self-esteem and lower the feelings of isolation. Take a look at what you are doing. Are you alienating yourself or your partner, and if so, why? Improving your self-esteem can improve virtually every aspect of your life, including strengthening your relationships and health. A life change due to health can be a common trigger for lowering how you perceive yourself. The challenge is to identify that this is going on and create an intimate connection to your partner at the same time.

Think about your behaviors and beliefs. Are they holding you back from intimacy with your partner? Consciously thinking positive thoughts can boost your self-esteem but it takes practice. The reality of your condition is based in fact, but how you approach it can make all of the difference. Start simple with words and reminders to yourself. Then reconnecting to your partner will become easier.

Rekindling the romance could be as simple as a few words, a gesture, and a kind of look or touch that will let the other person know you are ok. Be conscious of this each day so that not a day goes by without a kind word or gesture, even if you are not having sex daily. And really, who is when you're in constant pain? Try this the next time you are washing your hands at the bathroom sink, write 'I love you' on the mirror with a soapy finger or lipstick. This can help create an intimate moment.

Be the one to take control if your partner is afraid that they will hurt you further because of your current pain level. Be sure to reach out and let them know you would like to have a sexual experience. Say, 'Do you want to have sex right now?' or whatever cute, sexy, clever way feels natural to you. Lead the experience to relieve their worry.

Spouses often have different sexual desires. Turning your desire totally off just because of pain is causing harm to your relationship. Remember, hurt verses harm. Your partner married you expecting a healthy sexual relationship. Holding back on intimacy can lead to ending of the marriage or infidelity. The last thing a chronic pain patient needs is more discomfort. When sex increases pain and patients avoid sex or even coddling, the relationship suffers. Don't let this be the beginning of a vicious cycle of no sex.

What can you do to increase the connection, romance, and sex you are sharing with your partner? When you are having those talks in a neutral setting as I spoke of before, try to share your struggles with staying close. You can also share positives like sex helps you cope with chronic pain.

To increase the romance in your relationship you can try other forms of sexual experiences. Touch in any form increases feelings of intimacy between partners.

- Be creative with positions other than what you traditionally expect; lay side by side, kneel or sit
- One partner may use masturbation during mutual sexual activity if the other partner is unable to be very active
- Over-the-counter lubricants can help with pain associated to vaginal dryness (this can occur with a variety of medications and conditions)
- Plan your activities around your medication schedule so you don't further hinder your sex life
- Use oral sex as an alternative to traditional intercourse
- Vibrators can add pleasure without physical exertion

Real Love and Good Sex for Chronic Pain Patients and Their Partners

Root of Dysfunction

Emotional, physical, and medication factors all play a role in chronic pain patients dealing with sexual dysfunction issues. When a person is in chronic pain it changes their self-esteem as Barby talked about earlier. When a person's self-esteem decreases so does their sexual desire. Many chronic pain patients also are experiencing depression, anxiety, and stress which contribute to the loss of a desire to be sexual. Take steps to protect yourself self-esteem. To help communication with your partner you can use these techniques:

- Positive affirmations
- Understanding your pain condition
- Counseling
- Reading self-help books on positive mental attitude techniques

Pain by itself can cause sexual dysfunction. Many of the medications used to treat chronic pain diseases can also cause a lower sex drive, vaginal dryness in women or erectile dysfunction in men. When this occurs, talk to your provider about what you are experiencing so adjustments can be made to medications or counseling can be prescribed to help move past these challenges.

In my research preparing to write this book I was not surprised to find that one of the most common reasons people use to get out of sex is a headache. In 2007 a survey by the National Headache Foundation found that 69% of respondents said they had avoided sex because of a headache. As we detail in the next chapter, sex can actually help a headache. When chronic pain affects intimacy out of excuses, it is the relationship that suffers. Don't let fear of pain become habit. Remember, hurt verses harm.

Sexual dysfunction can come from habit as well. When people don't feel well on a constant basis they can get into the habit of not having physical contact with their partner. After a while the person in pain can forget to even think about the needs of their partner and become consumed with their pain experience. As humans we need physical touch and companionship. If you are falling into a pattern of a sexless relationship make a conscious effort to change the situation.

In chapter one I talked about the 5 stages of a relationship. When it comes to sexual intimacy there are 4 stages involved; desire, excitement, orgasm, and resolution. Desire is interest and the want for sex. This is often referred to as our libido or sex drive.

Excitement is a state of arousal that often occurs as a result of touching and kissing. This is the foreplay such as touching, kissing, and petting encouraging stimulation. Our bodies respond to the excitement by increasing the heart rate, blood pressure, and breathing in anticipation of the release of endorphins. Blood flow increases to the genitals of both men and women. Men become erect and woman begin to secret vaginal fluids.

In my opinion the best stage is the climax of the experience also known as an orgasm. During an orgasm muscles contract resulting in waves of pleasure throughout the body and a release of endorphins in the brain. As I reach an orgasm my body feels hot. I feel my private area pulsating and then there are a few seconds of exquisite sensations. Depending on the buildup there are multiple intense spasms or smaller waves, spaced less close together.

Finally, resolution is the return of the body to a state of relaxation and euphoria. Your stress levels are decreased almost like putting your worries on a back shelf of your brain, pain is not the first thought. It is almost as if your body has a reset switch.

Talking to your provider about your sexual activities can be nerve wracking and a bit embarrassing for many. Unless we speak up about what we are experiencing we will not find a work-around for whatever is causing the dysfunction. More than likely it is something that can be overcome if we just communicate. Even if you are embarrassed or shy simply describe the changes you are having; lack of desire, difficulty with performance. Just like when a patient brings in a list of medications they are currently taking and the benefits or side effects they are experiencing, it is important to have this sexual function discussion.

When it comes to living with chronic pain it is common that the patient will develop some level of depression. Why would you not when you're whole life changes. As well as the neuroinflammation levels increasing there are changes to the brain. Keep in mind that some of the medications to combat the depression, stress, and anxiety can also cause a lack of desire, vaginal dryness, or erectile dysfunction. Being conscious that these side effects may occur, you can address them easier if you are open about it.

Many times if the person in pain recognizes that this is the case, they can give themselves time to get into the petting and touching with their partner. They end up with the great benefits of the experience as well. If you think that your sex drive is not normal due to a side effect of a medication you are taking, it is important to speak to your doctor about it. Medications can also cause a lack of libido and vaginal dryness.

When your partner has a decreased sex drive due to medications they are holding you back from fulfilling your own needs. This is causing your relationship suffers. It could be fixed by something simple like switching up medications. Remember to tell the provider about any over the counter or herbal remedies the patient is using as they may be a factor as well. Your provider can check medications, hormone levels and may refer you to a sex therapist or an endocrinologist depending on what you are experiencing. If the patient is male, medications such as Viagra can assist in getting them prepared for a sexual experience. For women vaginal moisturizers are helpful for dryness and additional comfort.

Being open in your communication with your partner will make it more comfortable as you learn each other and the special needs to make it the best it can be. The more you discuss your concerns and desires the easier it becomes to please each other. Do not let embarrassment be a barrier. If you don't become comfortable stating your feelings in a manner that is loving and supportive it gets harder to do over time.

To get past the worries of pain start by touching one another. Giving each other a massage just to connect your bodies physically. Before you begin, set the mood to be relaxing and romantic. You can use music, lighting, and candles. Keep the room warm so it is comfortable to be naked. A patient that is cold and in pain will have a difficult time participating. Take your time and use your imagination to find positions that produce less pain. We had to experiment with positions, angles, levels, and support pillows to find what worked best for us. It does take time, but the more you practice, the better it becomes and the more fun it is for both of you.

In the beginning as you are getting comfortable and relearning each other in a romantic way, it doesn't have to lead to actual sex. You can find ways to pleasure each other and yourself using toys, lotions, and verbal communication to help build the connection. If you are having trouble being creative or you are shy, use books, videos and other resources to help you learn more about sexual health.

Real Love and Good Sex for Chronic Pain Patients and Their Partners

The Payoff of Orgasm

One of the most difficult things about chronic pain is the profound impact that it can have on your sex life. If you think you are the only chronic pain sufferer with intimacy issues, think again. "It's a silent epidemic," says Clifford Gevirtz, MD, medical director of Somnia Pain Management in New Rochelle, N.Y. "People are embarrassed to talk about it, but they are suffering." There are a lot of couples suffering unnecessarily because there is so much help available when it comes to sex and creating stronger intimacy with your partner. Talk to your partner first, if that is not enough talk to your providers. Doctors such as gynecologists, primary care physicians, and therapist can help if you only have the courage to ask.

From the start of my marriage with Ken I had decided, we would have sex anytime either of us wanted. Even when I was feeling awful I remembered that anyone can participate for 5-10 minutes with their partner and then you can go back to resting. You are going to hurt either way, you might as well have some bonding time with your partner to keep the sexual relationship healthy. One thing I found was that intimacy actually helped my pain, at least temporarily. Our doctors prescribes opiates for pain relief but one of the best natural opiates is an orgasm. Our brain produces endorphins when we have an orgasm and this helps bring our pain levels down. Even if only temporarily, the pain level is lowered. This works a lot better than many other treatment modalities we try, and serves the purpose of keeping us connected to our partner.

Are you still worried about how the pain will affect you afterwards or even during? Challenge yourself and your partner to be creative and practice possible ways to help you enjoy the experience of intimacy. If you are reconnecting with a long time partner be conscious of any long-standing ways of thinking and behaving. The long-held thoughts can feel normal but perceptions can change with a want and willingness to reconnect in an intimate and sexual way.

Remember it is not all-or-nothing. There are many levels and creative ways to have a sexual experience. If you have vaginal pain, opt for other types of sex that is still satisfying to your partner and keeps you close. There doesn't have to be penetration every time or even most times, but it should be satisfying every time. Commit to the time it takes to have the sexual experience and mentally filter out the negative pain for a few minutes. Don't reject your partner and positive experiences by insisting that any connection doesn't count unless it is traditional sex. Believe me, your partner will be happy to have an orgasm whether it is from oral, traditional or masturbation activities. Do not be shy about investing into your sexual relationship. These days it is very easy to be creative. For example you can get a lubricant that adds heat, tingling, or numbing sensations. Vibrators come in all sizes and styles and are an inexpensive way to add great benefits for both men and women.

Treat yourself and your partner with kindness and encouragement especially if it has been a long time since you have connected on a sexual level. Remember that negative thoughts can be a self-fulfilling prophecy. If you think you are going to increase your pain by having sex, you probably will and the satisfaction and endorphins will not be where they could be. Taking your time and working together to have a satisfying experience despite the pain can become a habit and you might surprise yourself and your partner. Try telling yourself things such as, "I can handle this. This is going to be a great experience with my partner".

Every experience is an isolated moment in time. Focus on the positive and think about the good parts of your body, partner, life, and feelings. Remind yourself that sexual experiences are an amazing way God gave us to connect to one another at the most intimate level. Sex is what separates family and friends from our partner in life. Nothing can bring you closer to another human being.

Encouragement for yourself and your partner goes a long way. In the beginning it may seem awkward but the sexual act gets easier with practice and communication. You will begin to recognize what can fulfil you and your partner with the least pain and most satisfaction. Then relax and let your endorphins work their magic on the chronic pain.

So you are not in the sharing mood or your pain levels are off the chart. Vaginal stimulation with or without orgasm can lower pain levels. According to Barry R. Komisaruk, PhD, a distinguished service professor at Rutgers University said, "vaginal stimulation can block chronic back and leg pain, and many women have told us that genital self-stimulation can reduce menstrual cramps, arthritic pain, and in some cases even a headache."

I have had horrible migraines that went on for hours with no relief from medication or meditation. When Ken would get home from work, we would engage in intercourse and within 10 minutes, my migraine would be gone or at least only now a headache. I am sure the foreplay of a gentle massage prior to sex only helped as well. It also helped relax me and allowed for better sleep. I have found that even touching and hugging can help me release my body's feel-good hormones. I can just feel the stress melt away.

For us women sex is a great workout for our pelvic floor muscles. For those of us with bladder challenges orgasms cause contractions in the bladder muscles. These contractions strengthen vaginal muscles which helps to correct bladder leaks. This is a common problem for women with chronic pain.

Having sex as little as one to two times a week can boost your immune system as well. We all know that a person in chronic pain has a compromised immune system from the stress the disease puts on our bodies. A research study at Wilkes University in Pennsylvania found that college students who had sex once or twice a week had higher levels of a certain antibody compared to those who had less sex.

The more you have sex the more your libido will improve, the more endorphins you will have, and lower pain levels will come more often.

For those of you reading this that do not have a life partner yet. Remember to be good to yourself first and that masturbation is ok. Not only is it ok to do, you can get the same benefits from orgasms if you are using a partner, a toy, or yourself.

Real Love and Good Sex for Chronic Pain Patients and Their Partners

Intimacy & Romance

Do you anticipate the pain? Do you just turn off your sexuality because intercourse may be physically uncomfortable? Are you just unwilling to be intimate with your partner because you are afraid they will hurt you?

I met my husband after I developed reflex sympathetic dystrophy. Even though a proper diagnosis was not given to me we didn't realize the magnitude this would have on our relationship. Over time we developed some understandings as to how I am doing and what positions I am able to do when at certain pain levels and depending on the location that the pain is worst at the time. We will straight out ask each other, "do you want to have sex", whenever one of us is in the mood. We try to take the complexity out of sex. When I feel emotionally unwilling or just physically am not up for it, we do a quickie. When I am doing alright and want to get the full benefits of a sexual encounter, we take our time and make it more romantic and involved.

Because I know how important sexual relations are to a marriage long-term, I take any self-esteem issues and check them at the start of the foreplay. I understand that this can be difficult. Just remind yourself this is your partner and they chose to be with you. If you are good enough for them to want to be with physically, then don't let your own emotions and thoughts get in the way.

I can see how someone who was the head of the house and is now confined to a wheelchair can be worried about self-esteem. How could you not be affected? My incentive to provide physical pleasure to my husband is so that our relationship is not like any other in my life. I want my husband to be connected to me in a way that no one else in my life gets to experience. I believe this helps keep our marriage strong and our goal to stay together easier.

I was worried that it would be impossible to develop a serious relationship being in pain day and night. I knew I wanted a relationship but also knew that I wanted to provide my partner with what they need. I didn't want to be alone forever and worried about how a partner would respond to my limitations. The first few years I always thought, this is a temporary situation. Over time we learned that dealing with pain would be a lifelong situation.

I remember Ken asking me out for the first time, and me thinking, what do I have to offer you? The thing is, Ken didn't know me and all I had done before. He only knew what was in front of him at the time. Once I got past my own insecurities and remembered to love myself first, it made it possible for me to love him as well. I had to remember our relationship wasn't about what I can and can't do. It is more who we are as people and how we can be with one another.

We practiced and learned to interact with each other. It goes back to the stages of a relationship Ken talked about earlier. We had to be friends first. Once we were friends and able to laugh at ourselves and each other the relationship grew. About this time in my life I realized that it is ok if I am not perfect. I don't have to accept the guilt that others try to put on me. I had to do what was right for me.

Ken had to deal with similar issues. A few members of his family were not too keen on the idea of him dating someone who had limitations. One of the biggest limitations was that I was unable to have children due to endometriosis. When I met Ken he knew that this was the case and had said he didn't want children so that helped us in our decision making. The pressure from his family was strong for him to have children. Even though it would have been us taking care of them which is a huge task and responsibility we didn't want and weren't able to do.

Once we were able to form and storm we were able to norm. Norming is when the intimacy really kicks up a notch. We had passed the awkward stages and were accepting of the other with all of our faults. Each knowing that this was our choice. Neither of us was in the relationship as a crutch, out of guilt others were putting on us, or desperation. We are a untied team.

The relationship was able to thrive and grow as we increased intimacy and romance. As life through curve balls at us we began to appreciate the irony, and used it to get closer instead of letting it come between us. I remember Ken used to tell me I was a black and white thinker. I believe he was right. I believed that women should take care of the house, husband, etc. I was then too sick to keep up and I learned that nothing has to get done right now.

When you leave something for tomorrow because you simply can't do it today, it usually works itself out. Also, that cleaning didn't need to happen every day. Especially in a house with two adults and no pets or children. He was a person who was spontaneous, thrill seeking, and could live life in the gray areas. It is true when Ken says, "90% of what we worry about doesn't happen."

Overtime while increasing our intimate relationship we began to see we had different perspectives and ways to accomplish our dreams. Working at it together made our life moments that much more fulfilling. We had learned that being willing to be willing goes a long way in the romance department, strengthening our friendship and intimacy. Being willing to look at things from another perspective gave us the ability to resolve most challenges. Taking the time to stop and communicate with each other without putting emotions into the situation was a benefit.

Have you ever thought, if I had only taken a minute to listen I wound be in a better spot now? We found that if we have an important subject to talk about that we had to be sure to get our partners attention before starting. Speak up and say, can I have a few minutes?

Can you put down the remote, turn off the TV, get off the phone with your friend? I want Ken to feel loved and important. Keeping our marriage strong and us bonded is a high priority for both of us. We communicate with each other about all of the parts involved in a sexual relationship. Even down to the time of day. Usually we feel better in the morning or night. What body position will be best for the given day and how our body is doing is important. Reconnect often by exploring each other's bodies. This doesn't have to be specifically for the goal of orgasm, but more of a sense of connection and emotional intimacy. The following are actions you can take to raise intimacy levels and strengthen your relationship:

Do to your partner what you want for yourself – Do things that are specifically intended for your partner's pleasure. Show them that they are loved and appreciated the way you would like reciprocated. Find out what they would enjoy and do what you can to fulfil those needs as well. Let them know you are attracted to them and appreciate all that they do to make your life better. It shows them you are open to their affection and willing to give them attention.

Don't tempt good people – Ken has constantly told me this. I see it in regular life. It's that living in black and white vs color perspective. I lived in black and white for so long I didn't realize that the world is full of color. What is morally right for one is not necessarily right for the other. Without trust it is very difficult to be intimate. Make it a habit to check in with your partner and never give them any reason to doubt your loyalty and love.

Keep a healthy lifestyle – don't just consider what you are eating, drinking, smoking, or if you are using good hygiene. Be sure to add intimacy and romance into your healthy living practices. Even when your pain levels are high, intimacy is very important. Take a few minutes now to keep something great going far into your future. I know how easy it is to forget this aspect with so much else to deal with.

Lean on your partner first – When you have a challenge or situation you should be in a position where you want to call your partner first. It feels good knowing that they will be there for you when you call. It shows their commitment is to you and your relationship, over any other relationships the two of you have.

Set a goal – start with we will have sex at least 1 time every X days. Having a day to look forward to can be exciting in itself.

Touch each other – hold hands, sit next to each other to watch TV, etc. I have found that there are fewer disagreements when we are more affectionate with each other even when it is not an intimate moment. It is harder to argue with someone your holding hands with. Just touching in a kind way can help your partner know that you are on the same side and you support them. You just may have a different opinion they need to hear.

Take preemptive steps – If you see that there is a consistent issue coming up or that your partner is getting frustrated over an issue you should take the time to be proactive. Just like we take the time to stop and ask our providers if the plan we are on is still the correct path. You should take as much stock in your relationship. This will help you have a longer lasting relationship with your partner and keep you on the right path. It is far too easy to veer off the path and head up our own mountain.

Real Love and Good Sex for Chronic Pain Patients and Their Partners

The Other Side of Intimacy

As a caregiver I work on taking into consideration how Barby is doing. I learned to deal with my worries about what physical intimacy may do to her. For me it all came down to the vow 'in sickness and in health'. By the time I married Barby we knew she had a disease that was going to be a lifetime of challenges. I had to make my vow sooner in the relationship than most partners. I took it upon myself to examine what I wanted in a relationship. I knew that no partner would have everything going for them. I never knew her when she was totally healthy and pain free but I had seen her decline over the years bringing me to realize that verbal communication has to be a part of intimacy.

Many times if I am in the mood for an orgasm, I will ask, "Do you want to have sex"? That's what we have come up with. Very rarely does she say no. When she does, she offers me a time that it will be better for us both. Something of a response like, "how about tomorrow just before you leave for work?" This way she can rest after I leave and we are both satisfied. If she said no at the moment she is good about giving an alternate time. For us, we have also found that foreplay can get to be too much. If she spends all of her energy on foreplay there won't be much left for the actual act of sex. Other times we choose to do something intimate like petting or kissing, that doesn't have to lead to sex but just helps us keep our closeness. Having a chronic illness takes its toll on the whole family. Looking at the situation together has helped us create and maintain our strength as a couple.

When couples don't keep lines of communication open it leads to feelings of distance and the connection cant grow. I suggest that you take the time to talk about the illness and challenges but also keep other aspects of importance to each other in focus. If life is all about the illness, that is too much. If it is never discussed, that is not enough. Finding that middle ground will help keep the stress of the illness lowered.

With Barby there were places on her that I knew to never touch, whether we were being intimate or not. These chronic illnesses affect you each day and can vary greatly. We try to take advantage of her good moments in these times. If she was having a stressful time or sad, I knew that providing some intimacy such as just holding her hand while watching TV was a great way to connect. On days when she was doing better, I knew we should take advantage of the situation and get more intimate. Working on the coping skills for pain can give you tools to access when it comes to getting intimate with your partner.

I have to ask questions when needed. Sometimes the ability to think clear when pain levels are high is hindered. I would get mixed messages from Barby about what levels of intimacy she was ready to participate in. Until I learned to check for her cues. Things like is she talkative, is her eye drooping, has she been in bed all day with the lights out, or is she up watching a movie or mentoring another patient on the phone. We learned to be clear and direct with what we want and need because as we all know – we are not mind readers. Having a partner who has a chronic illness often shifts the power balance in a relationship. The more responsibilities I had to take on in life the worse the imbalance would get.

Knowing that caregiver burnout can happen pretty fast we both watch out for the signs. We know that putting too much stress on the partner for chores to get done was something we could let go further down the timeline. There are times when I would get sad, depressed, want to isolate myself, all signs of emotional and physical exhaustion. When I would get overwhelmed it helped me to think about all Barby was going through and how she was fighting everyday just to get through moment to moment. Knowing that she was continuing to fight for me, our relationship, and her own health help me get through these down times I experience myself. The irritable side of me would begin to creep out and I realized quickly that I had to take care of myself physically and emotionally before I could be there for her. It is like being on an airplane and the oxygen mask falls. They tell you to put your own on first. Then you can assist those around you. It is not being selfish to do this, it is allowing you to take care of your partner better because you will be stronger.

As suggested earlier, make a date in advance for sex. Setting the intimate time can help the situation and set the mood. Having a partner who is willing to try new positions and experiment as to what feels the best is important. Being funny and quick witted I help the intimate moments move along. If I suddenly feel the urge to get into a new position or I see Barby is struggling with the position we are in, I will stop for a switch up. We talk quickly make a decision and then get back into focusing on the great experience knowing that we are in a position that we will both enjoy.

I encourage Barby to keep going and remind her that she can rest afterwards and that the endorphins will help her feel better. It will all be worth it. Strengthening intimacy helps break down the emotional wedge that can build up between a couples. We know that emotional problems can exacerbate stress and pain. We have to keep it real to keep our relationship strong. Be in the moment and let the stress of the condition, finances, self-esteem issues go. Believe me, they will be there when you get done. We all know that being positive about situations that are unpleasant to deal with can help us get through them easier and with less angst. Become aware of your needs and your partner's needs. Know that they need the emotional intimacy just as much as you do. Otherwise it is harder to have and keep the connection it is just human nature. Barby needs the love and affection just as much as I do and for this moment in time we can keep our mind off of the pain. Remembering this helps me increase satisfaction for us both and helps me satisfy my own intimate needs.

Find Your Sexy

You're still sexy with chronic pain and your partner still desires you. What you need to find and maintain is a comfortable sexy intimacy level. This intimacy can be explored and cultivated through petting, masturbation, exploring your partner, oral sex, sexual intercourse, different positions, role playing, sex toys, and lubricants.

Having actual intercourse is just one way to create closeness. Being sexually creative is a way to enhance and satisfy your intimacy needs. Things such as holding hands, cuddling, fondling, massaging and kissing increase these intimacy feelings. If you are unable to be very active, your partner may use masturbation techniques during your mutual sexual activity.

The bottom line is that intimacy and sex should be fun. The contact you achieve while having sex can help you be stronger. The intimacy you build with your partner will help you both cope better with your chronic pain.

Finding your 'sexy' doesn't happen overnight there is no magic to it. There is only practice and letting go of your so that you can experience the pleasure in the moment. For those who keep practicing to be sexy you will eventually develop a genuine affection and renewed love for your partner and your own body. Talking with your partner is the first step in reclaiming your sexuality.

Do you need help going from talking to the next level of intimacy? Practice discovering each other through touch. Eventually build up to what is best and most comfortable for you without having to think it through with the lights dimmed or off. One day you will realize that you are not practicing anymore, that intimacy comes natural and easy.

Learning to stay sexy, intimate and connected is like learning a new language. At first you are nervous, timid, maybe even scared to verbalize the words or practice them with others. The more you practice the more confidence you build. In the beginning you are comfortable speaking to your teacher but don't want others hearing you mess up. By the end you can go out in public and speak to others who know that particular language. Now, I know that you are thinking I am saying go share your sex life with others. Really, I am saying everything you do is awkward at first and then gets easier to the point of full comfort between you and your partner. It just takes time, love, respect, and encouragement. Fairytales don't happen without effort. I challenge you to create your own fairytale.

When trying to raise the love and intimacy between the two of you, do things that will make the other feel loved and appreciated. Start with emotional intimacy. Let them know that you are attracted to them, that you appreciate all they do for you and that you are open to their affections. Learn more about what makes your partner feel good, and reconnect with an exploration of each other's bodies, not specifically for orgasm, but a sense of learning about each other all over again. Figuring out what you find sexy and what makes you feel sexy is subjective. I am going to give you a few suggestions I came up with, but feel free to use your imagination and develop your own list. Sexy is an attitude and a feeling, everyone has the ability to obtain it.

Finding your sexy – actions for women in pain:

- Be unpredictable and expressive (in a loving manner) with your partner
- Being naked when alone and in front of your partner
- Drinking wine (if it doesn't interfere with your medications)
- Engage in a little friendly sex talk with your partner
- Get your hair done or try out a new nail polish
- Play with a popsicle or lollypop in your mouth
- Tell yourself that you are sexy (practice until its natural)

Finding your sexy – actions for men to help their partner feel sexy:

- Encourage her to feel good about herself often (not just before you want sex)
- Flirt! be friendly and honestly interested in her, and act like you enjoy spending time with her
- Give her compliments about more than just her eyes or smile
- If she can handle it give her a back or foot massage just to make her feel good
- Make or give her something that shows you love her (doesn't have to be big, just from the heart)
- Making her smile will increase her confidence
- Remember to say I love you, spontaneously (not just when hanging up the phone or leaving for work)

Finding your confidence – actions for men in pain:

- Groom yourself daily
- Keep your sense of humor
- Make her feel needed
- Stay in shape as best you can

- Tell yourself that you are sexy (again, practice until its natural)
- Understand your condition and help your partner understand what you are challenged with and develop ways to overcome it

Finding your confidence – actions for women to help their partner feel wanted:

- A simple touch brings out a man's confidence
- Always tell him he is the best
- Find him sexy: even if you aren't finding him sexy at the moment, but you love him pretend you do find him sexy
- Flirt with him
- Give him the look that says I want you like never before because each time it's better and better with our continued love
- Praise and thank him for his accomplishments
- Show him you want him

Real Love and Good Sex for Chronic Pain Patients and Their Partners

Pleasure Positions

Pleasure positions when you live in constant pain are important. There are some techniques you can use if you have intercourse with a chronic pain patient. This chapter will talk about some possible solutions to having a successful sexual experience for you and your partner. We listed some ideas for patients who have pain in upper or lower extremities and full body pain. We hope that there are some examples listed that help you have maximum pleasure despite the pain. Most importantly, let the person in pain have the control of choosing the position or activity, at least until you learn from each other and what works best for you.

Women remember if you are dealing with vaginal dryness due to a medication complication or an inability to get aroused in the excitement stage due to pain, using a water based lubricant, and lots of it, will help the experience be more pleasurable. A study done a few years ago funded by Indiana University, found that women who used lubricant while having sex reported significantly less pain and got the benefit of much higher levels of satisfaction. The following pages are ideas that are helpful in jumpstarting the creative process and are positions that can be pleasurable for both partners.

Woman on Top Facing Away

Facing away from her partner who is lying down. The woman can move easily and stimulate herself by hand (or toy) if she wants. This gives the woman control of the situation and the man must rely on her decisions.

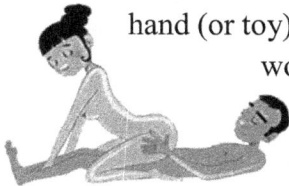

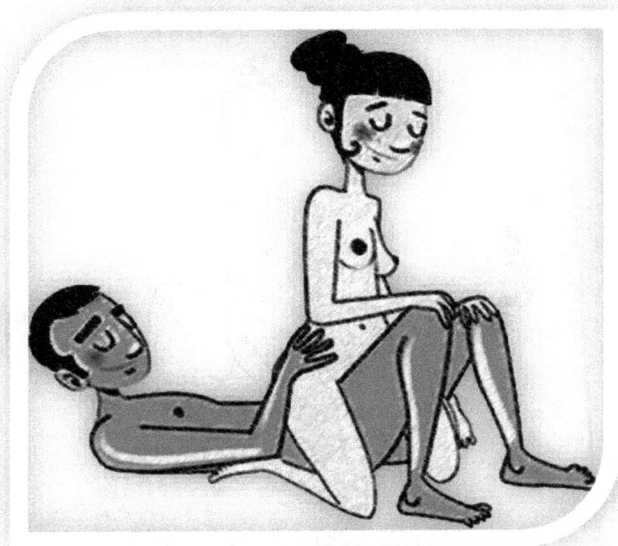

Woman on top facing away
using his knees for support

Facing away from her partner who is lying down
with his knees up. The woman can move up and
down easily and can hold the man's knees for
support. This gives the woman control of the
situation and the man must rely on her decisions.

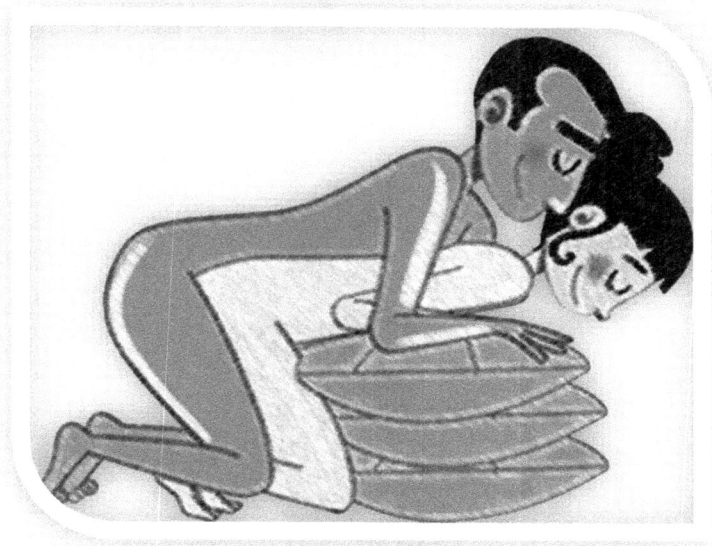

Adapted Doggie Style

The woman faces away from her man, holding herself up with her knees and arms or piling pillows to hold her upper body. The man kneels and straddles her from behind. This position is also good if the partner has issues with too much touch. It is also good for deeper penetration.

Standing Man

The man stands behind the woman. This position is best when partners are nearly the same height. For deeper penetration the woman can lean forward. The male is now able to stimulate the breasts or genitals from this position. If you have an issue with touch you can lean forward for minimal contact. If the woman needs help with balance stand in front of a wall or a sturdy chair that you can hold onto.

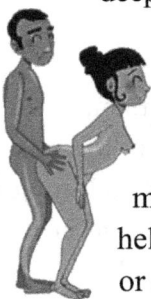

Adapted Standing man

If the partners are not the same height the standing man position can be adapted. The woman faces away from her man kneeling on a chair or edge of the bed. The man straddles her from behind. This position is also good if the partner has issues with too much touch. If you have a home with stairs you can find different heights and levels to get a variety of positions for both of you.

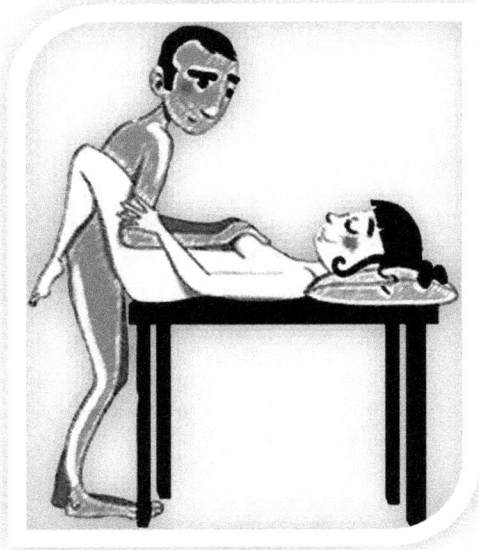

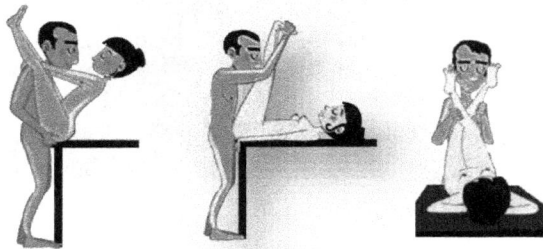

On the Edge

From a standing position the woman lays back onto a sturdy surface. The woman straddles the man and can avoid touching legs or use her legs to pull him to her. Motion can come from the man or woman. The woman can lean forward into the man and gets clitoral stimulation with penetration. Motion can come from the man or woman.

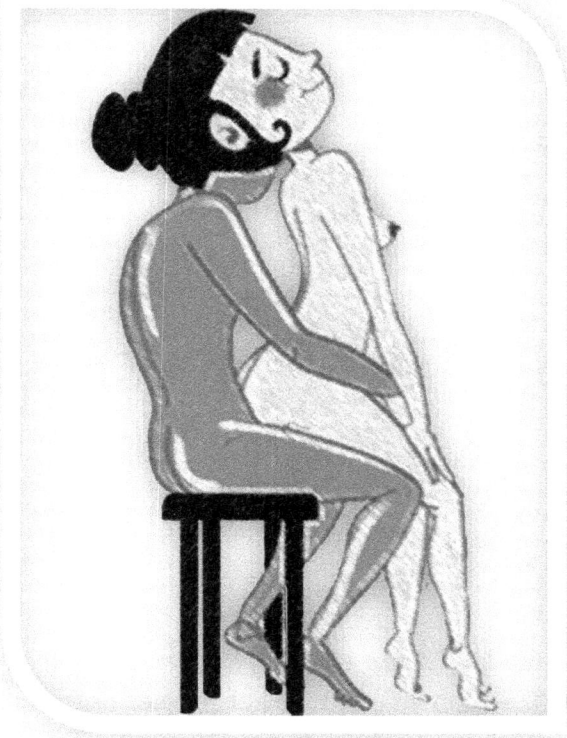

Sitting Pretty

Sitting on a sturdy chair, the man positions his feet on the ground with his feet apart. The woman sits on his lap facing away. The woman can use his knees to balance if needed. This avoids leg touching. The woman provides motion while the man relies on her decisions.

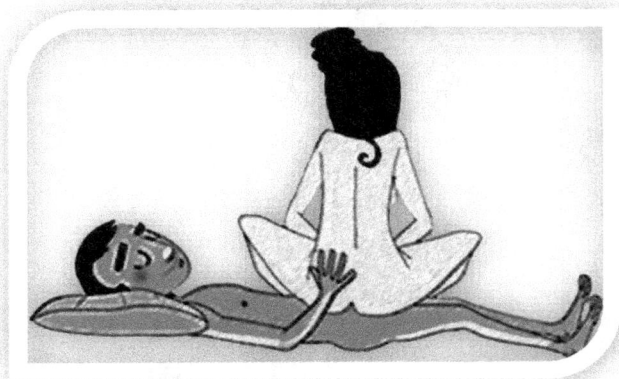

Woman on Top

The man lays down straight. The woman sits on the man. The woman can face her partner or turn to the side which changes the feeling for both. The woman can move up and down easily. This gives the woman control of the situation and the man must rely on her decisions.

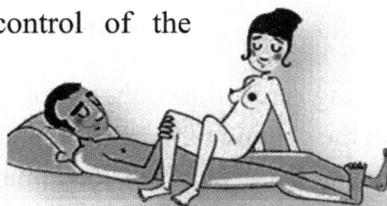

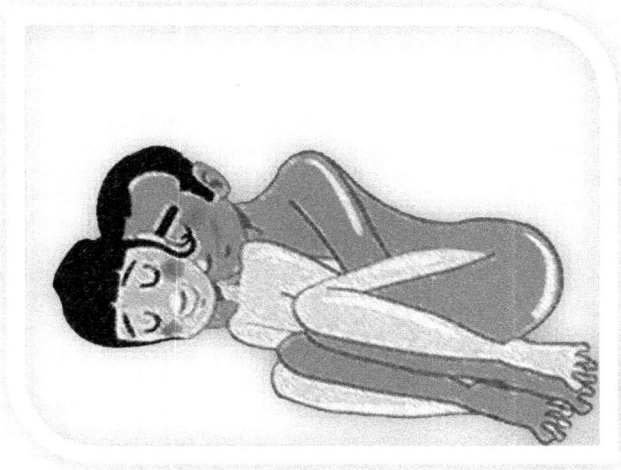

On The Side

The woman lies on her side with top leg bent. Man snuggles close on his side behind his partner. The more the woman bends her legs forward the deeper the penetration.

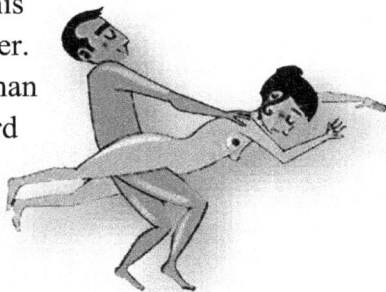

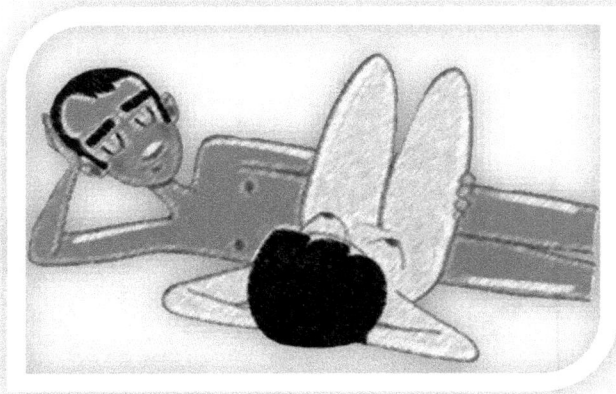

Ceiling Fan

The woman lays on her back looking up at the ceiling and lifts her legs over the partners' hips. To keep the penis in the vagina keep your legs bent. Movement can come from one or both.

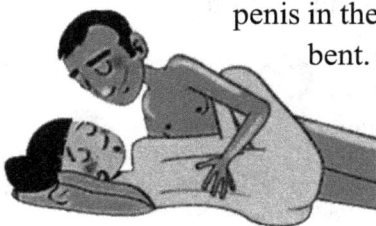

L Macho

Woman lays on her side with her legs extended. Man leans over her and enters facing her. There is little contact with legs and feet. Man holds himself off of the woman for less body contact.

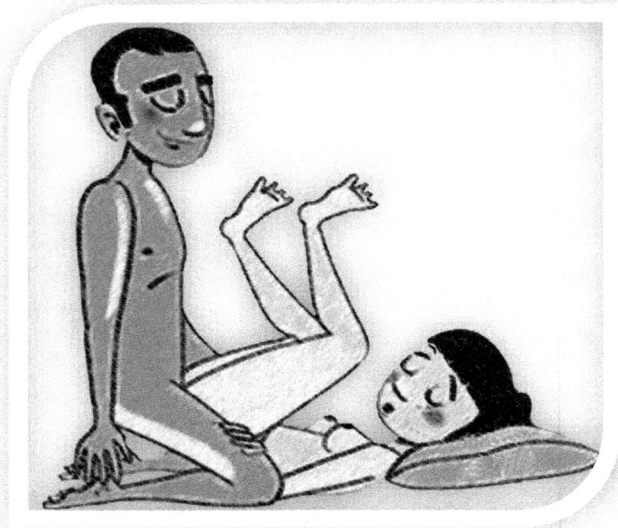

Bendee

If you need to elevate your feet have the man kneel
facing you. The woman bends
her knees up, rotating the hips
into place. If your legs can't
hold themselves up, rest your
feet on your man's chest.

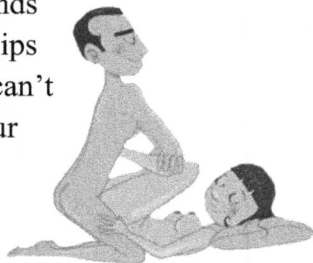

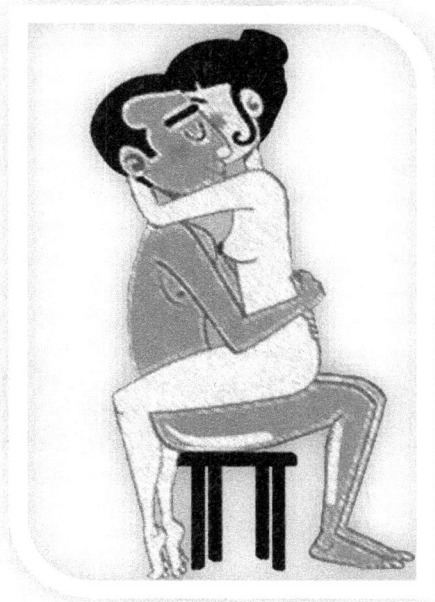

Glider

Man sits on bench with legs together. Woman mounts man facing him. This is good for close body contact during intercourse gliding back and forth for pleasure at her own speed.

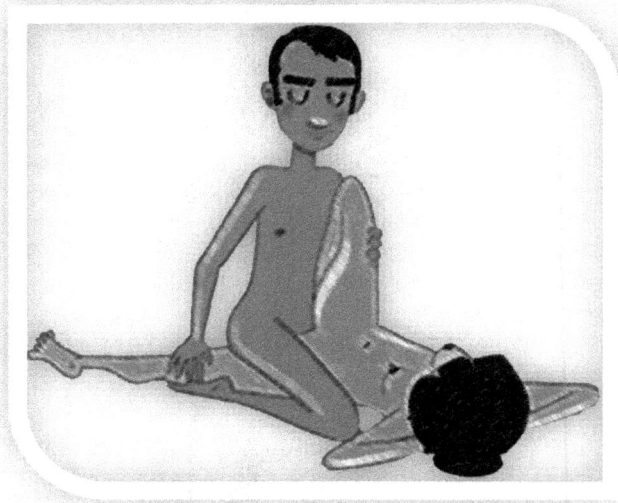

Sit and Slide

Woman lays on her back with one leg straight and pulls the other leg up to her chest so man can get into position. The man kneels into the crotch of the woman and can hold her leg. The woman's leg can also drape over the man's shoulder if needed. This position is good if you have trouble with upper body contact.

It is great to fall in love,

but better to feel someone else

fall in love with you,

flaws and all!

Real Love and Good Sex for Chronic Pain Patients and Their Partners

Other Books by Barby Ingle

Barby's books are for all of those suffering from chronic pain as well as their family, caregivers, healthcare professionals and public. Until you feel the pain, it is difficult to understand the challenges it brings on even after remission is successfully reached. Her books put this into great perspective with easy to follow and understand information. Whether a person is dealing with physical or mental pain, it can and will consume you if you allow it to. Only the patient can begin the process of healing, and Barby's wish is that these books will inspire the patient's eventual transformation filled with HOPE.

www.barbyingle.com

www.powerofpain.org

ReMission Possible;
Yours If You Choose To Accept It

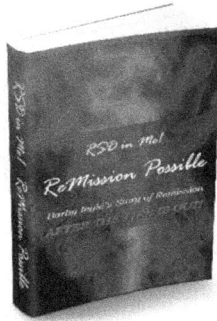

A valuable look into the process of healing socially, emotionally and physically after remission is achieved. Life does not just go back to the way it was before your illness. Recognizing this and moving through it can help you adjust to the new life that you now face. This book is about a patient's journey, (one year leading up to an IV-Infusion treatment that put author Barby Ingle into remission and one year of what happened after) of health, social; and mental adjustments. ReMission Possible is a follow up book to RSD in Me but also stands alone as a story that you too can achieve. It is a motivational guide to being your own best advocate, "The Chief of Staff of Your Own Medical Team" as Barby likes to say. All of Barby Ingle's books are wide reaching with one in three Americans dealing with a chronic pain condition of some sort.

The Pain Code; *Walking Through the Minefield of the Health System*

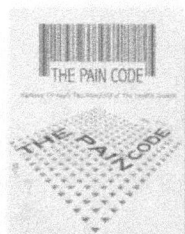

When it comes to living, the best life you can when faced with a chronic care condition every person has choices. It is a matter of finding the right fit for you. The patient can either let the disease run them or sort through the system and take control of the disease. Coping with a chronic condition takes hope and self-awareness. Through the author's struggles and finding her way through the health system for the past 10 years, she gained knowledge that she passes on to the readers of this book. Topics covered include types of pain, depression, become an expert on your illness, organize your healthcare, treatment options, financial challenges, disability resources, challenges with insurance, finding community, create your oasis, and living well with chronic pain.

The Pain Code; Workbook and Journal
Supplement to the book

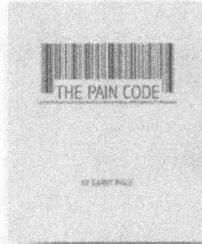

This is designed as a supplement to *The Pain Code; Walking Through the Minefield of the Health System.* This workbook-journal will help you discover how to talk with your providers. It includes sample insurance company appeal, medical record request letters and organizational information become your own best advocate. Getting organized is very important. It takes work in the beginning but it gets easier over time.

RSD in Me! A Patient and Caregivers Guide to RSD and Other Chronic Pain Conditions

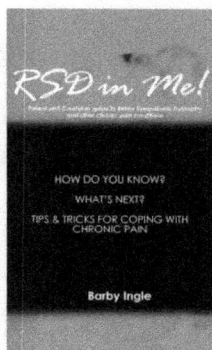

This book goes through aspects of Reflex Sympathetic Dystrophy (RSD/CRPS) and chronic pain including definition, causes, tips on working with healthcare professionals, emotional aspects, caretaker information, of dealing with chronic pain and tips on coping with the pain. The author based this book on her personal experiences in dealing with chronic pain and the healthcare system. Topics cover a wide range; history, causes, symptoms, getting a proper diagnosis, psychosocial aspects, treatment options, change in family dynamics, spirituality, working with the healthcare industry, helpful tips to use every day and more. As an amazon best seller this book continues to touch the lives of many patients, caregivers and providers. Proceeds raised from the sale of this book go to the funding of patient grants and awareness projects for the foundation.

The Wisdom of Ingle;
Fall Down and Get Up In Half a Day

The Wisdom of Ingle will give the reader a Satisfying Reading Experience. This book was started as a unique way to learn about our family history and share life lessons through our personal experiences. The book covers five generations of the Ingle Family History through parables and short stories. The book has clear-cut messages and likable characters with whom they can identify with easily. Each story tells and solves, a clear-cut narrative problem which the main character solves by his or her own efforts. The personal touch to each story makes the reader glad they read it, therefore giving the reader a Satisfying Reading Experience.

www.ingramcontent.com/pod-product-compliance
Lightning Source LLC
Chambersburg PA
CBHW060402050426
42449CB00009B/1869